Once there was a girl called Susie.

This was not so unusual, as she was
 only four years old and
most people are pretty small when
 they're four years old.

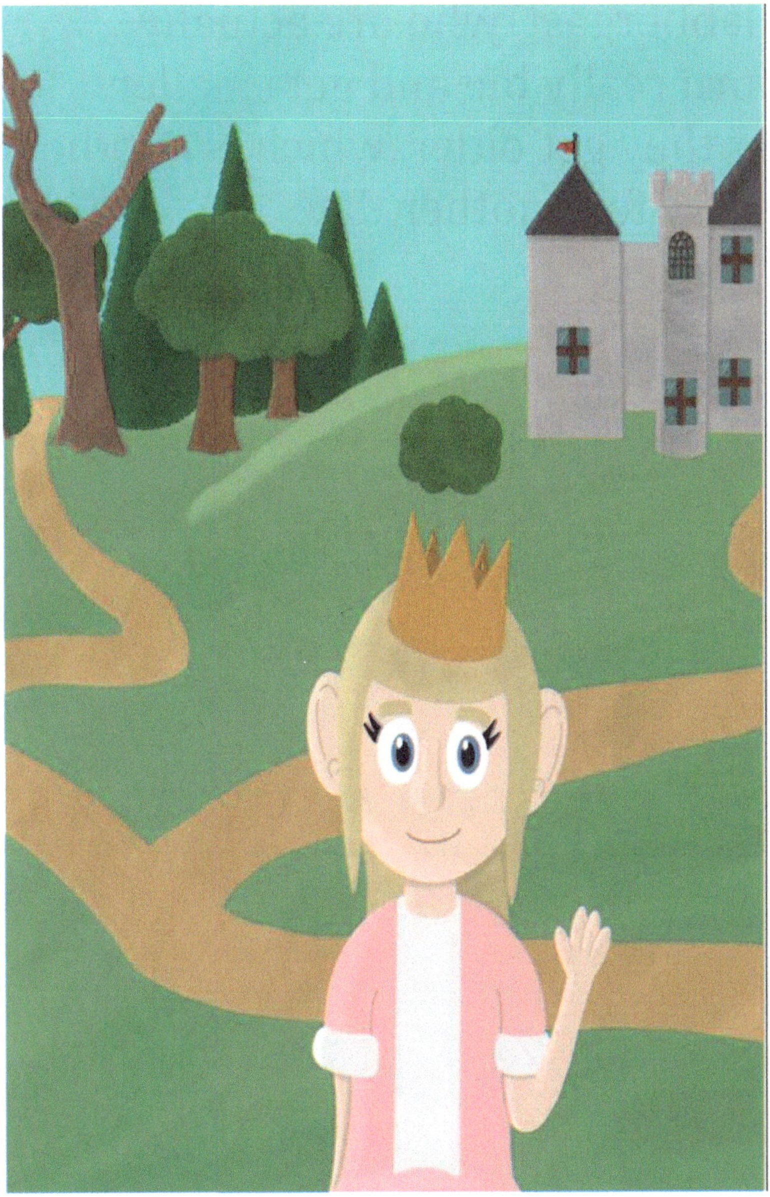

Notable exceptions are giants, elephants and Flittering Flabbergast, who are actually born really big and get smaller as they get older, which is another story for another day.

This story is about something different, but i've already
forgotten what that was, so let me just read back over what
I've already written to remind myself.

Oh, right. Susie,
Susie wanted a baby brother more than she wanted
 cake which is a lot!) so she asked her Mom and Dad
 (who, by coincidence, were a Queen and a King) if she
 could have one.

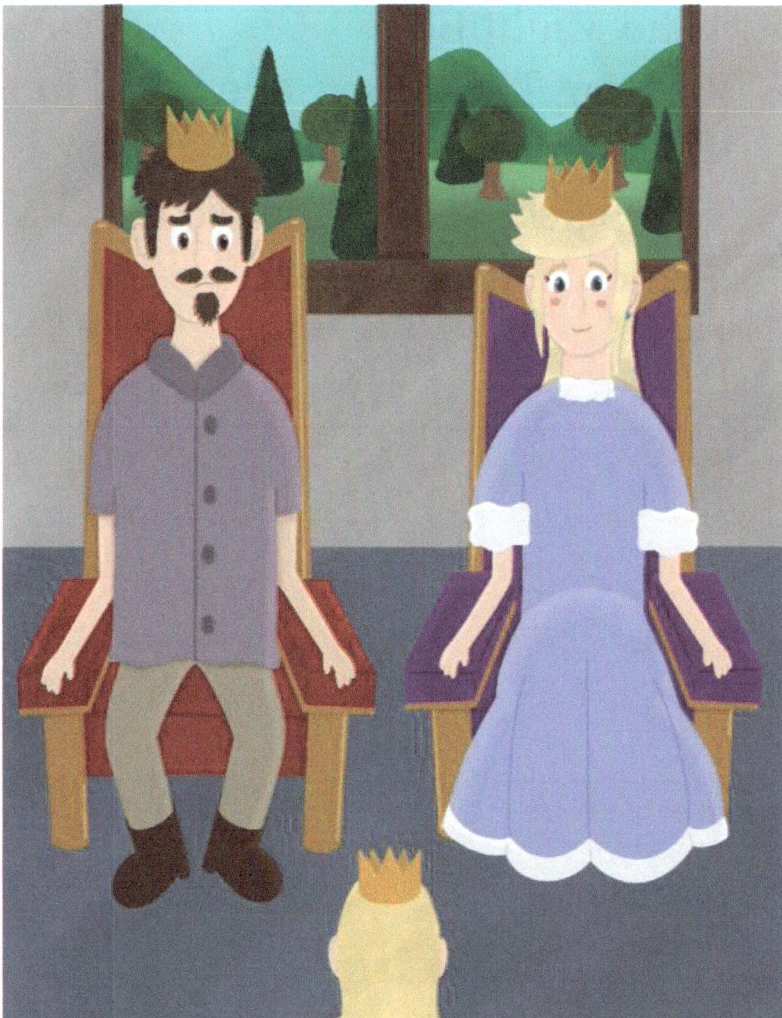

"Well... we'll see."
Believe it or not, Grown-Up Types Who Might Be
Reading This Story, every kid in the universe knows what
"we'll see" means and so did Princess Susie.

So, she went to see Gus, The Wizard Who Lived In A Bush Just Outside The Castle.

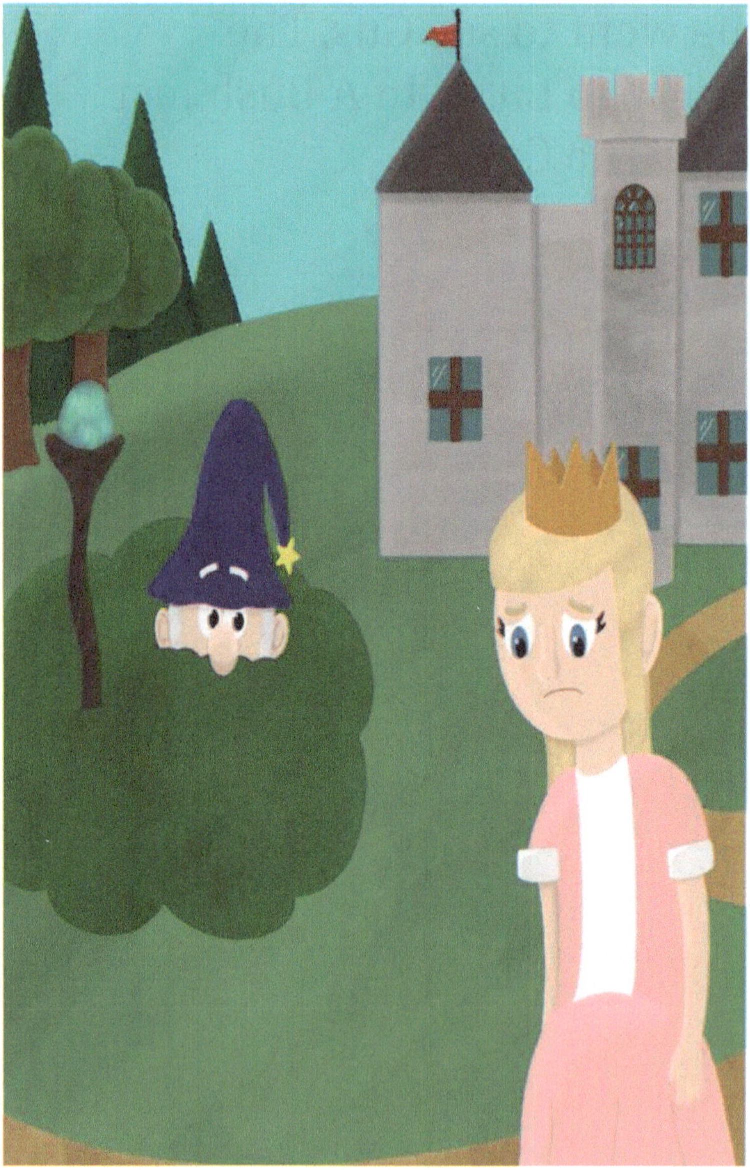

My baby brother, eh?" said Gus from behind a clump of leaves.

"That's tricky. But it can be done. If you walk into the Big
Scary Forest until you find the Bunny Tree.

Give the Bunnies
an offering and they will give you
a Magic Compass which
will lead you to Tiger Cave.

There you must solve the Tiger's Riddle. If you fail to answer
the riddle, you'll be eaten up.
But if you guess right, he'll give you a seed.
Take the seed home and plant it in a small pot of soil.

Be super nice to the pot of soil for two days, then put it on the windowsill and you will have your baby brother."
"Okay!" said Susie. And she turned to set off on her adventure.

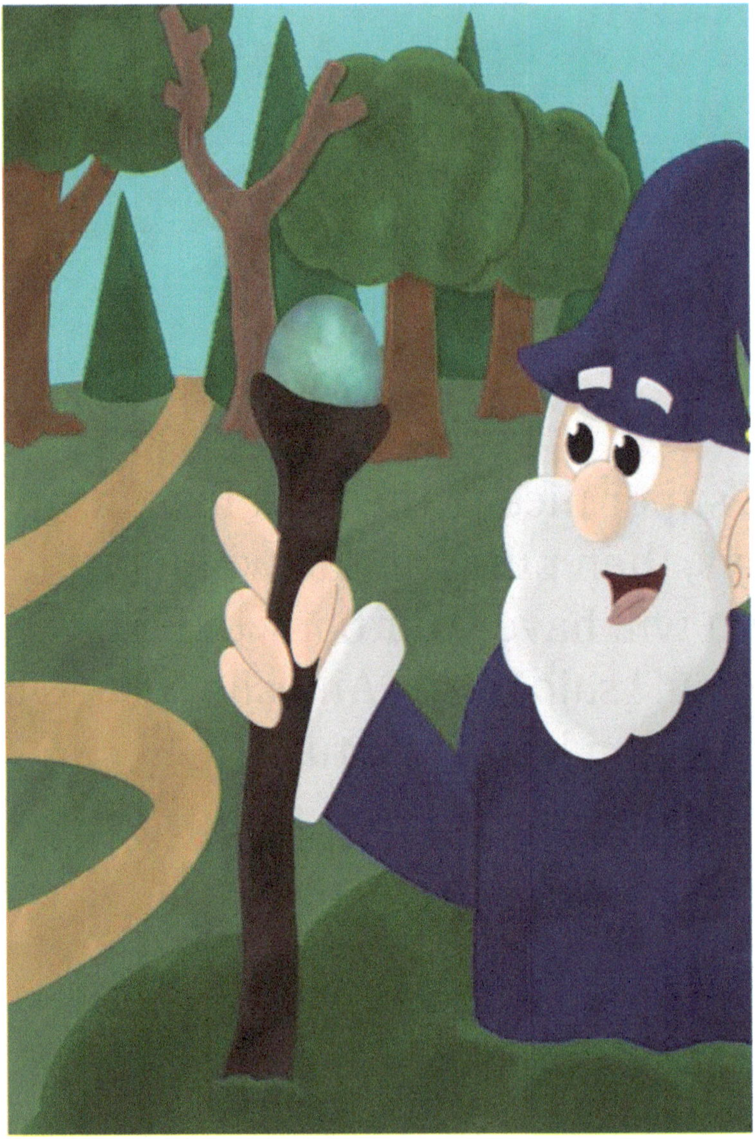

"Wait!" cried Gus.

"You're a four-year-old girl! You can't go on such a dangerous journey by yourself!"

"Oh. Okay," said Susie, and went to see a friend of hers. Tyrone was a Milk Man, which is another way of saying he owned a cow and sold her milk to people.

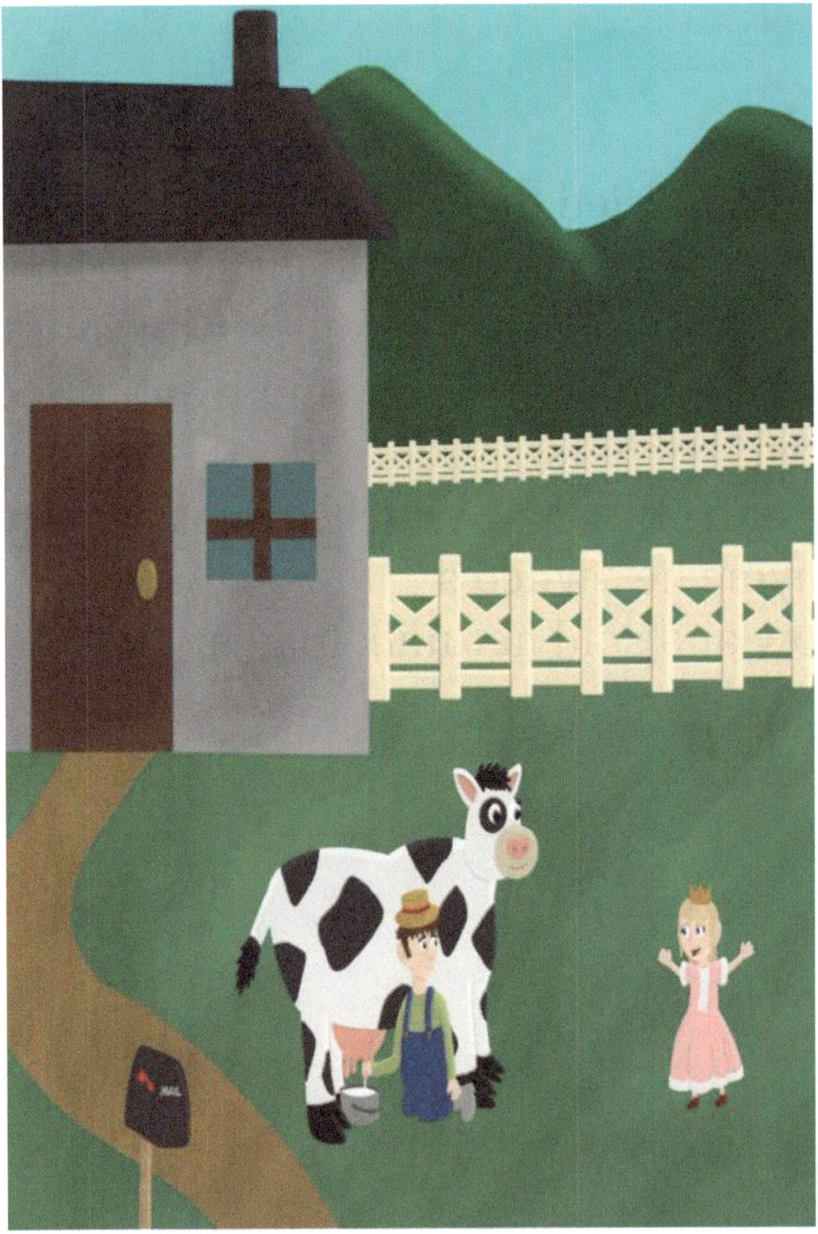

"Tyrone," said Princess Susie. "Will you come on a dangerous
journey with me?"
"Yeah, all right, said Tyrone.
And off they went on their adventure:
Susie, the Princess, Tyrone, the Milk Man, and Estelle, the Cow.

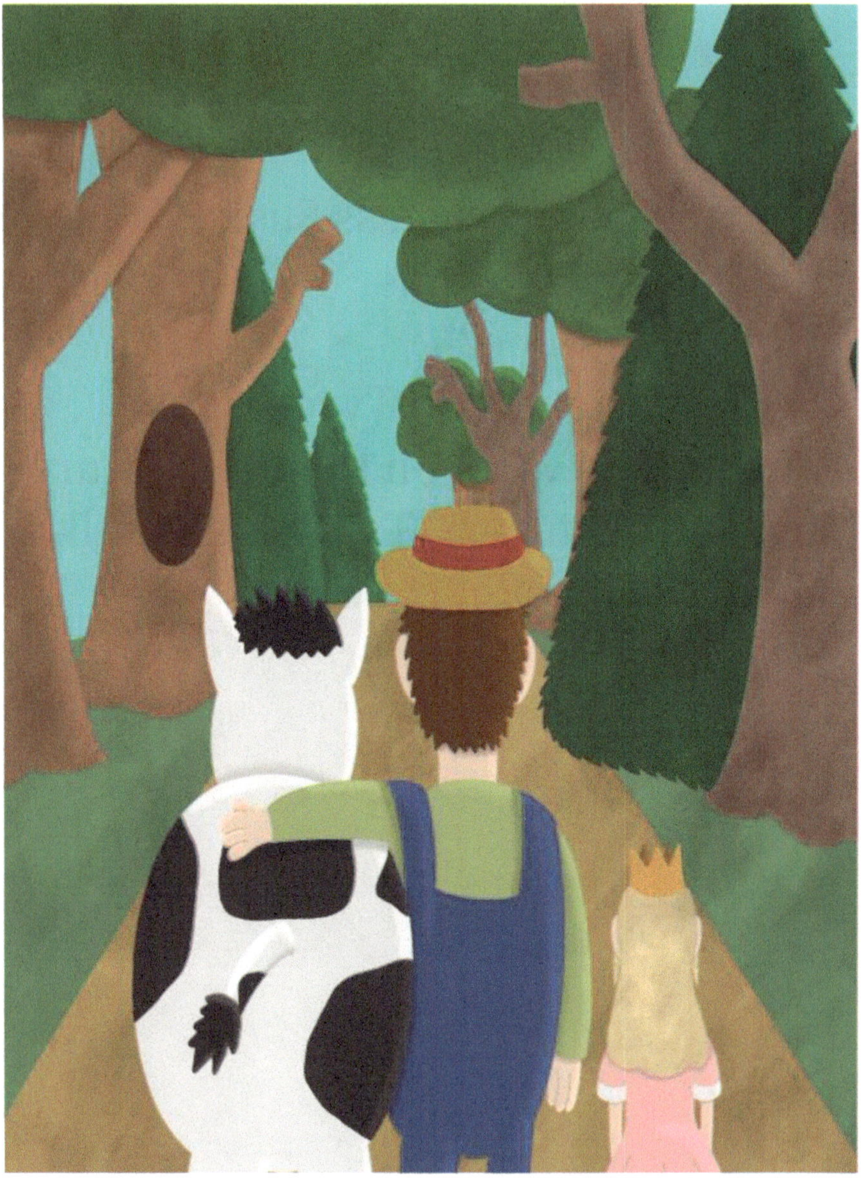

The Bunny Tree was located in the very center of the Big Scary
Forest which was really only Scary
at night time, though it was still pretty
 Big, and still a Forest). It was a large, lopsided, overgrown
fir tree.

And it was called The Bunny Tree because a warren of bunnies had made their home under its branches.

"Hi, bunnies!" said Susie when she and her companions arrived. Upon hearing this greeting, several bunnies poked their heads out from under the tree, looking at the Girl, the Man and the Cow.

"I'm Princess Susie and I have an offering for you.

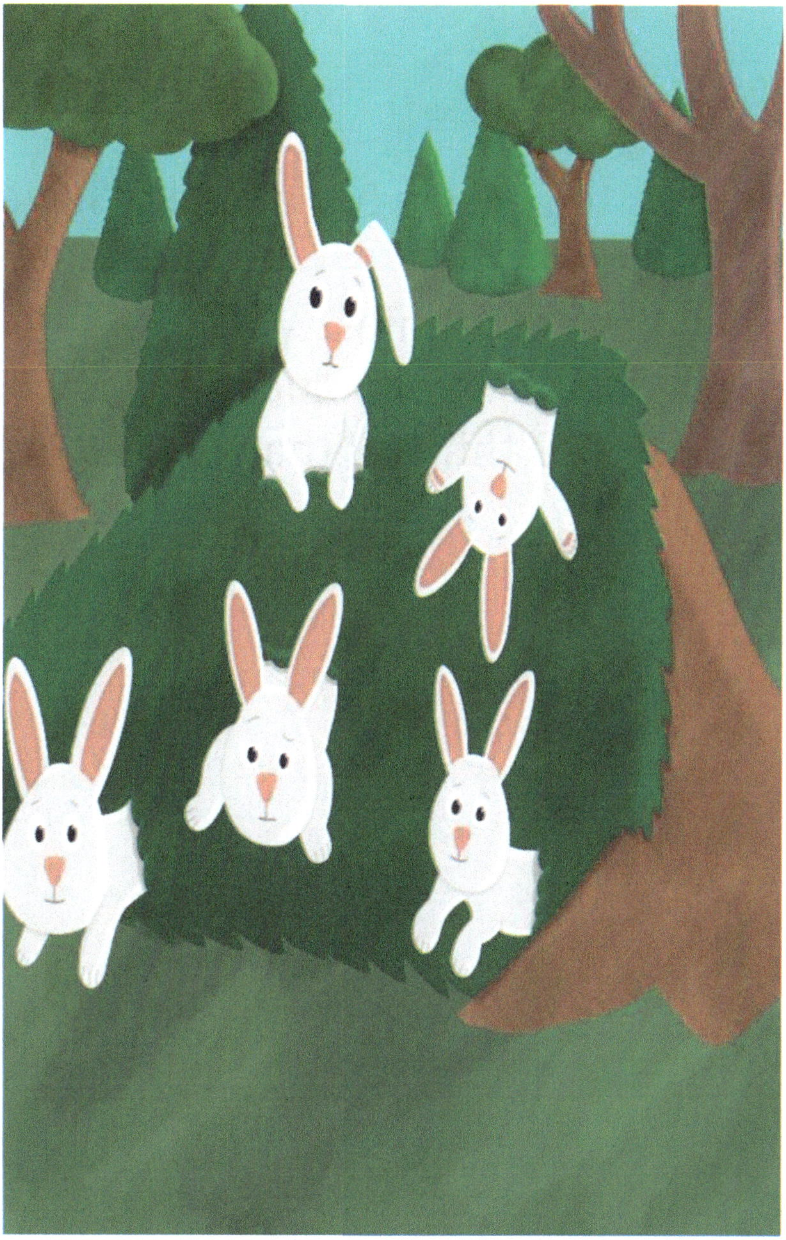

Who wants to guess what offering Susie brought? Carrots?
Because they're Bunnies? Well, no.
 It wasn't that. It was cookies.
What made you think of that, Susie?

"I figured everybody else brings them carrots," she explained, "so they might like something different for a change." She was right.

The Bunnies seemed very pleased with the cookies
 especially when they paired it with some of Estelle's milk)
and happily gave Princess Susie the
 Magic Compass.

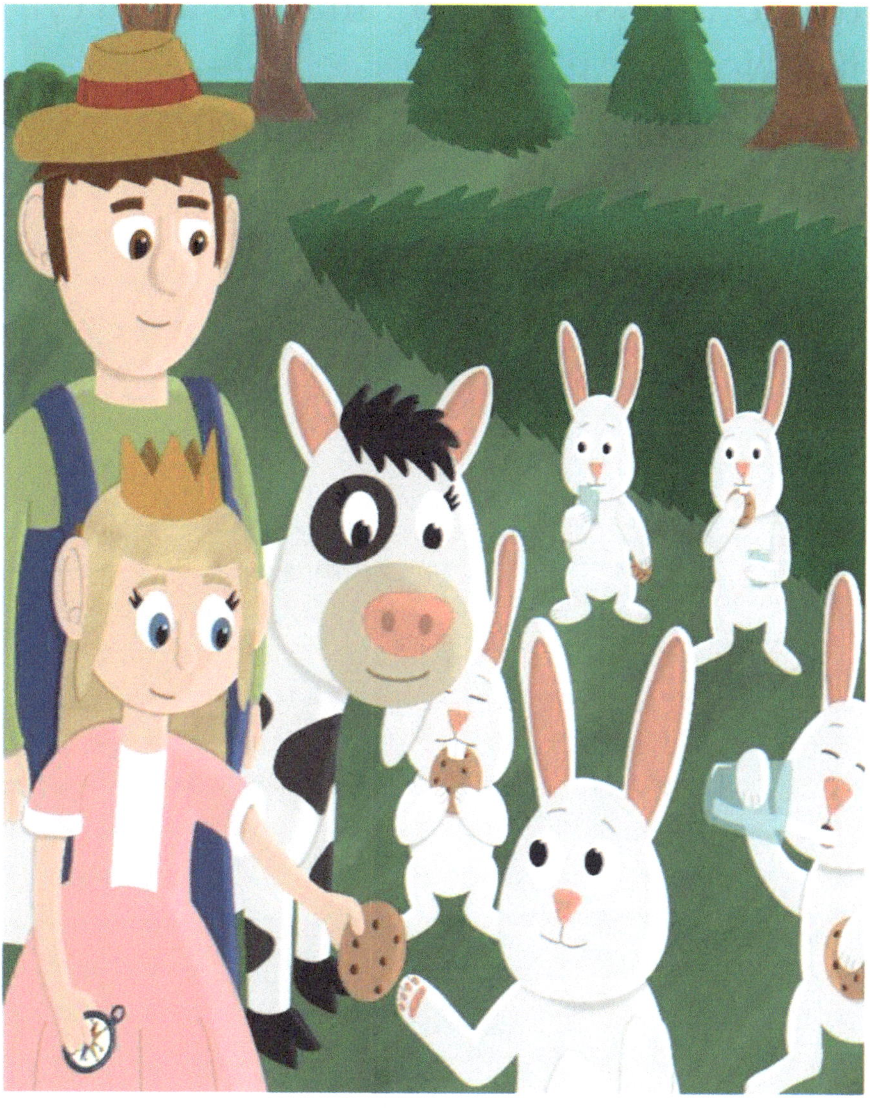

Most compasses, as you may be aware, point North. All
 the time. No matter what. Which is why it gets very tediously
 being a compass.

But this compass, this Magic Compass, didn't point North.

It pointed to the Tiger Cave on the other side of the Forest.

Susie, Tyrone and Estelle were about
 to go in when a deep,
booming voice from within said
"Only one may enter!

"I better go," said Tyrone. "'Im the adult here."
"No," said Susie. "It's my quest. I need to do this"
"But, Susie.."

"No! I'm a princess and I order you to stay out here with
 Estelle. And, Estelle, I order you to stay out here with Tyrone.

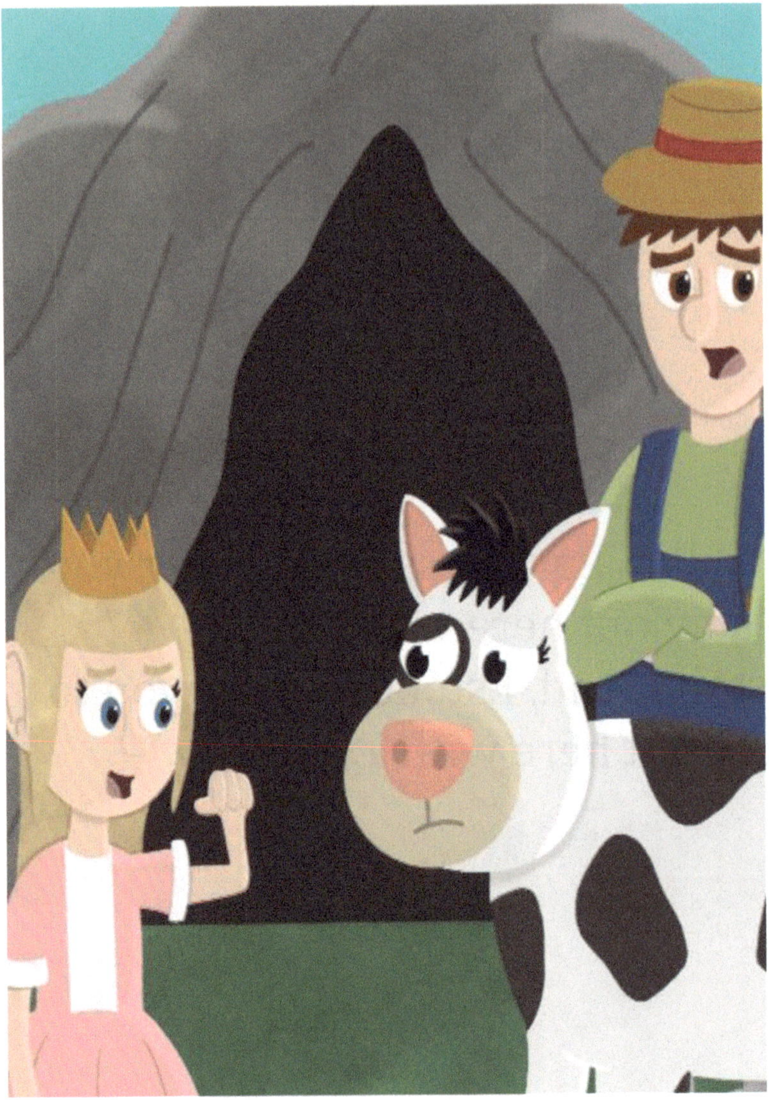

So, saying, Susie entered the cave, her head held bravely
aloft. Once she was inside, the entrance to
the cave sealed
behind her so that neither Tyrone nor Estelle could go in. Soon, Susie was alone with the Tiger of Tiger Cave .

"Hi, Tiger!" she said.
"If you answer my riddle," said the Tiger, " will grant you
whatever you desire. If, however, you fail to answer, I
will eat you up.
Do you accept the terms of this deal?"
"Um...okay!"

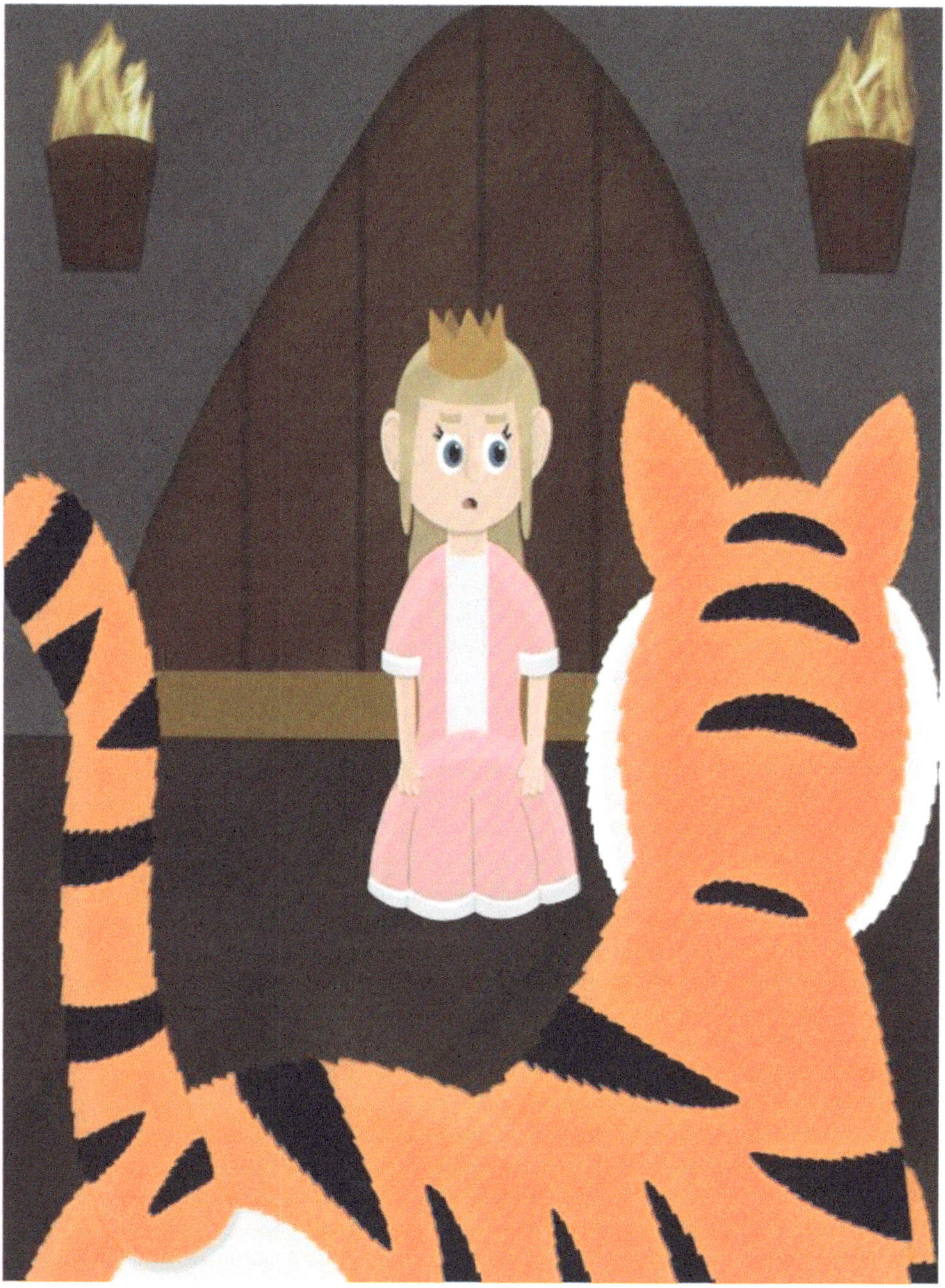

"Very well. Here is the riddle:
In the summer it's cold, in the winter it's hot.
But it's not what I have, but what I have not.

No legs and no arms, but fingers and toes,
Too cold when the sun shines, too hot when it snows.
I make not a sound, but they all hear my words.
And I fly like a cheetah and run like the birds.
What am I?"

Princess Susie thought and thought and thought as hard
as she very well could. But she did not know the answer to
the riddle (And neither do I, so please don't ask me.)

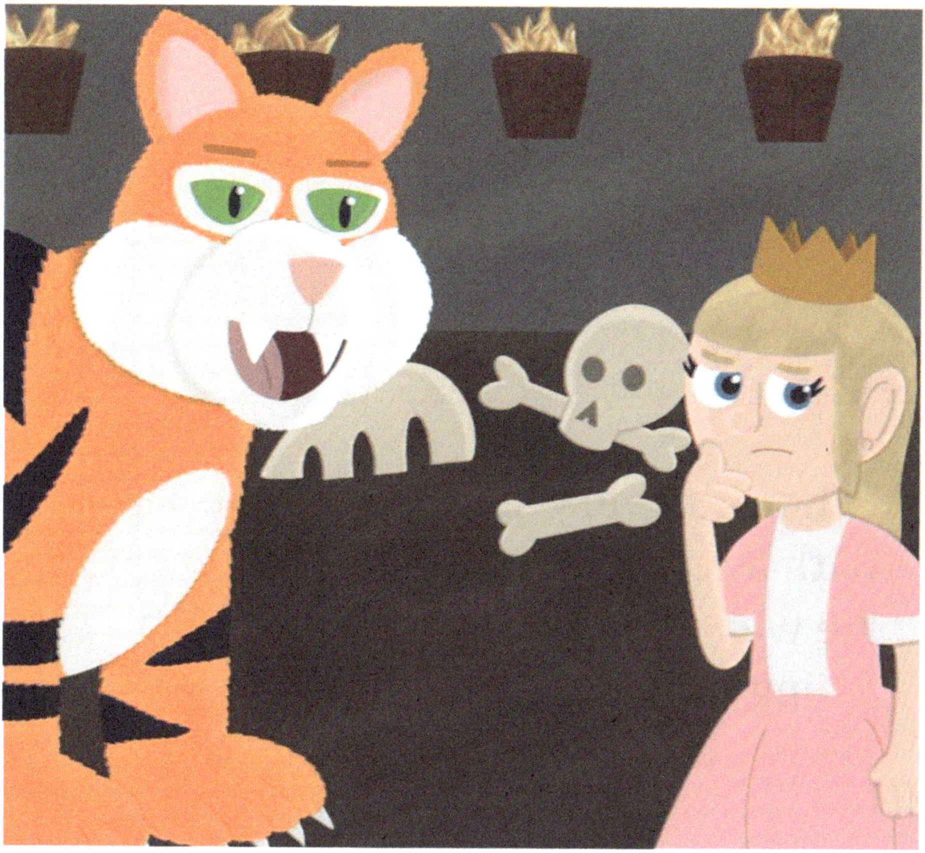

"Then, I'm very sorry," said the Tiger, with a grin that indicated
 he was not all that sorry, "but I'm going to have to eat you
 alive now.

"Before you do, can I ask you a question?"
'I suppose."
"Can I have a hug?"
"A what?"

"One last hug before I die. I've never hugged a tiger before.

"Come to think of it, no one has ever hugged me before.

People tend not to hug tigers.
They either try to kill us or
they run from us. But never hug.
Okay, why not?"

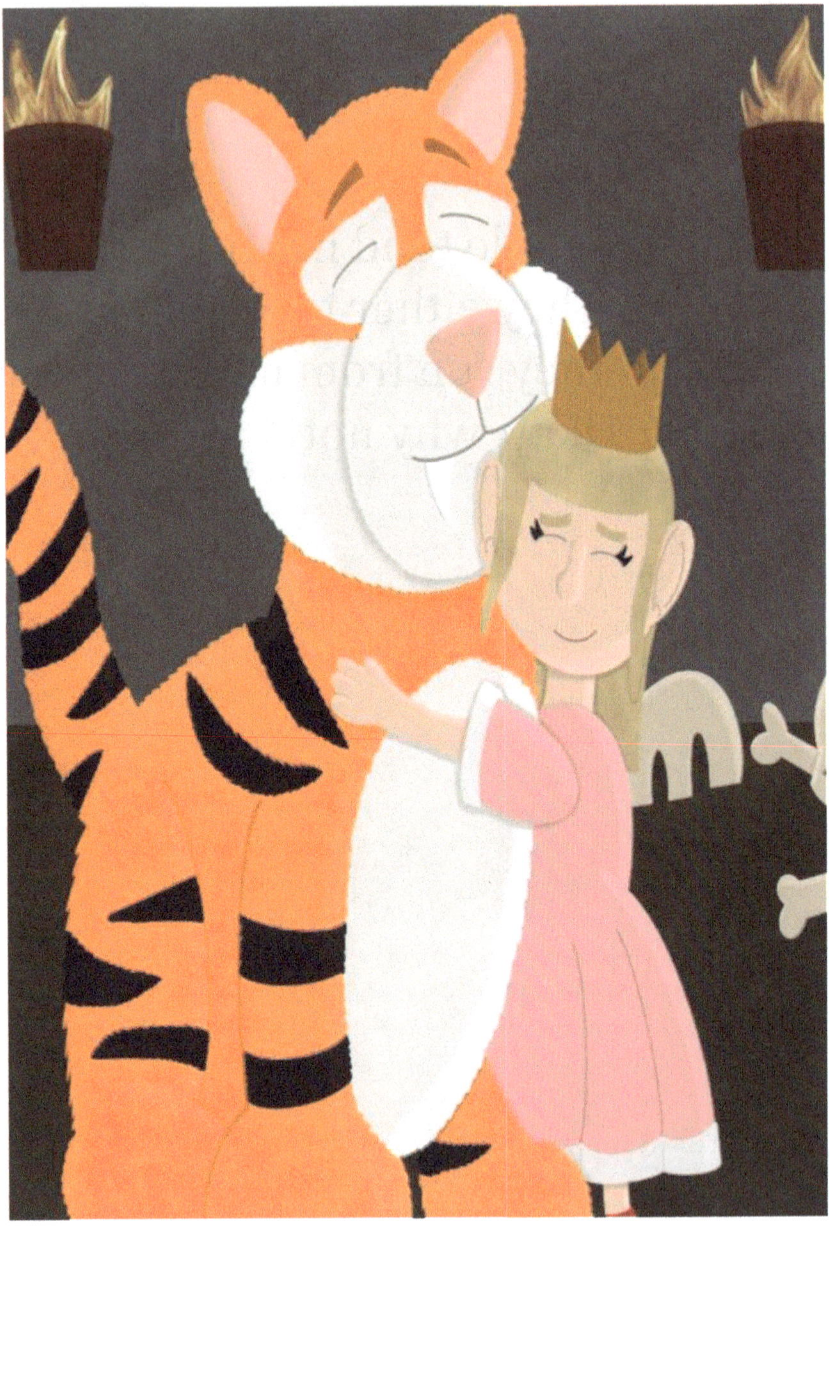

And Princess Susie gave the
Tiger.
 the Biggest, Nicest Hug
That A Tiger Ever Got.

"Hey! This is pretty good! I Like this way better than
making people answer riddles and eating them if they get it
wrong. Thank you, little princess. You know what? I'm
going to give you what you want anyway.

"And not eat me?"
"Right. And not eat you. So, what'll it be?"
"My friend Gus, who lives in a bush, told
 me you had a
 seed that I could use to grow a baby
brother."

"Oh, yes, I have that somewhere. Let me see...where did I
 put that? Oh, here we go.
There you are. Farewell!"
"Bye, Tiger!"

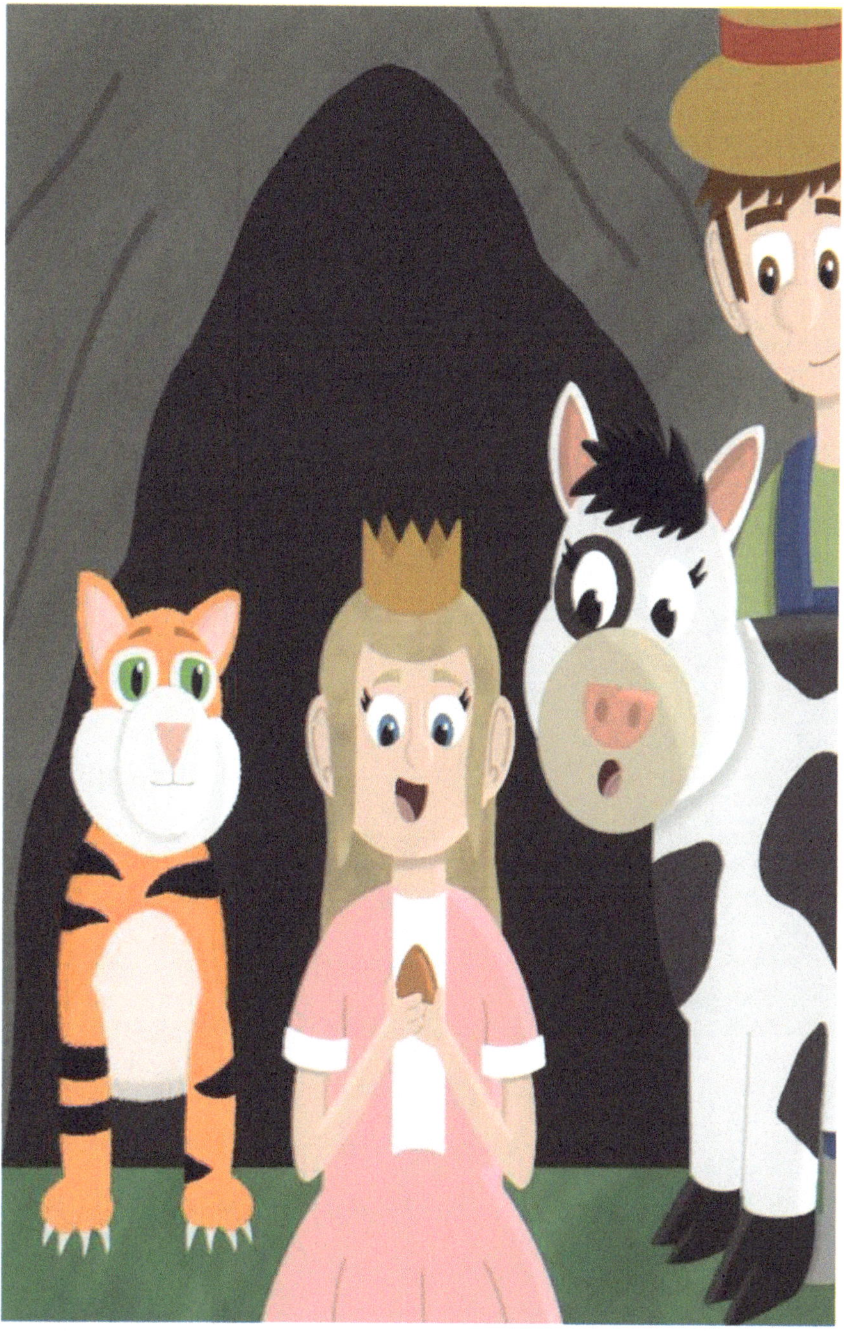

Tyrone and Estelle walked Susie back to
her castle. On the
way, she told her friends what had happened between
her and the Tiger. They both agreed that it was pretty amazing."That's pretty amazing, said Tyrone."Moo,' said Estelle.

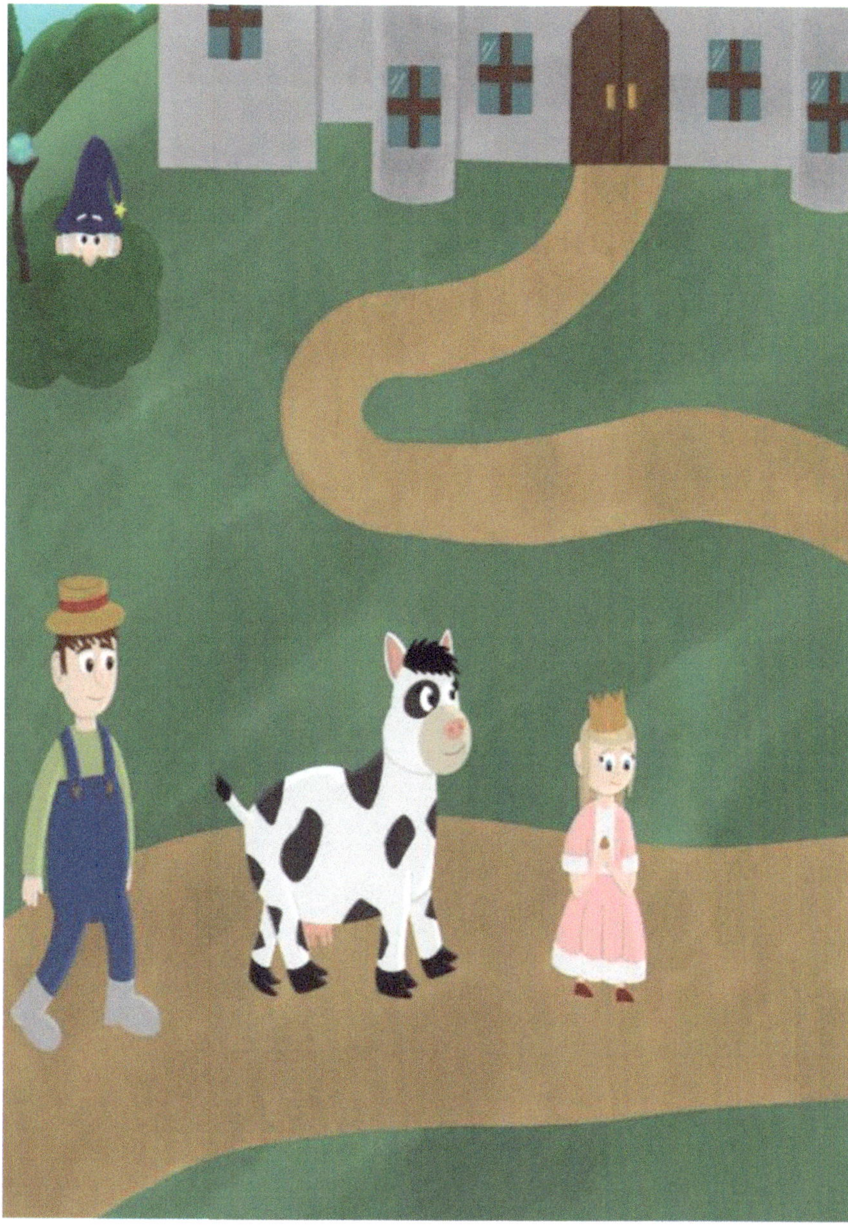

After saying "buh-bye" to the Milk Man and the Cow, Susie went to see the Royal Gardener, Ruth.

"Can I have a pot with some soil in it, please?"
The Royal Gardener, Ruth, gave her such a pot, and Susie
planted the seed inside. She then spent the next two days
being very nice to the pot.

Playing games with it, telling it stories, talking to it.
She named it "Bernard."

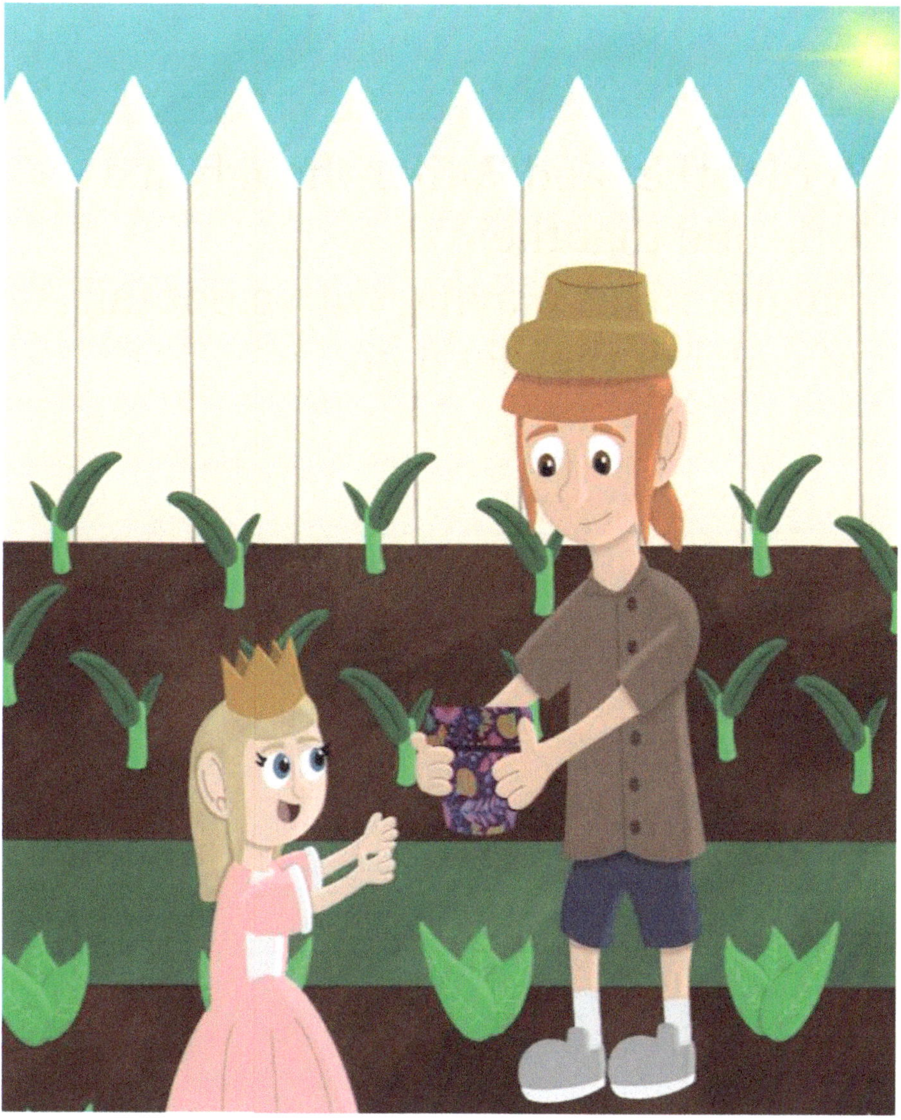

Her Mother and Father thought it a little odd that their
daughter was playing with a pot full of soil, but they let it go.

It's not actually necessary for parents to understand everything
their kids do, as long as they're safe and happy while doing them.
After two days of unremitting niceness.

Susie put the pot on her windowsill, gave it a good night kiss
 and said, "Nighty-night, Bernard, then went to bed herself.

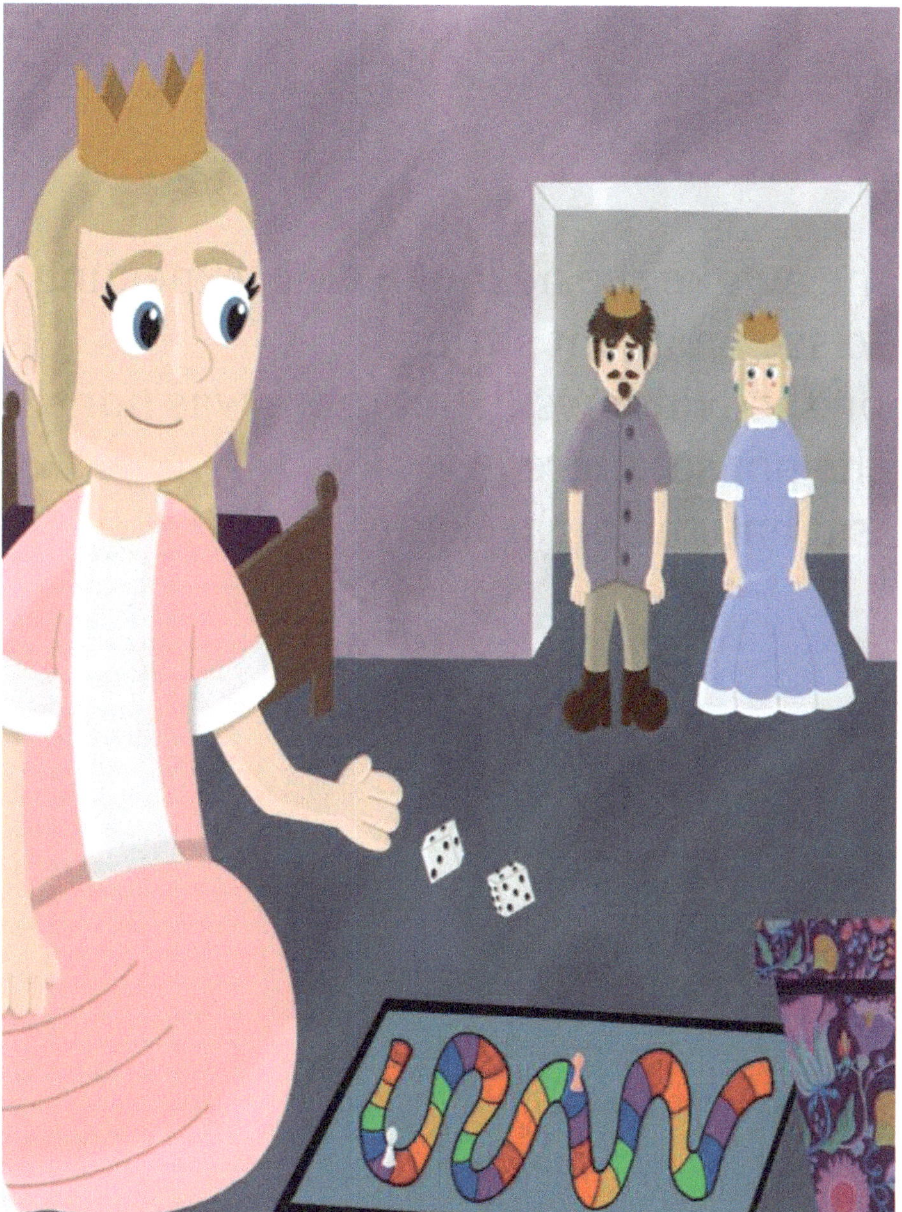

She awoke the next morning, expecting
 to see an infant sitting
  on the windowsill, but there was none.
The pot sat there just
as it had the night before.

Princess Susie was very upset, even more so when she dug around in the soil and found that the seed was gone! She thought a bird must have come in the night and eaten her baby brother.

So, it was a Very Sad And Despondent
Susie who came
downstairs to breakfast that morning.

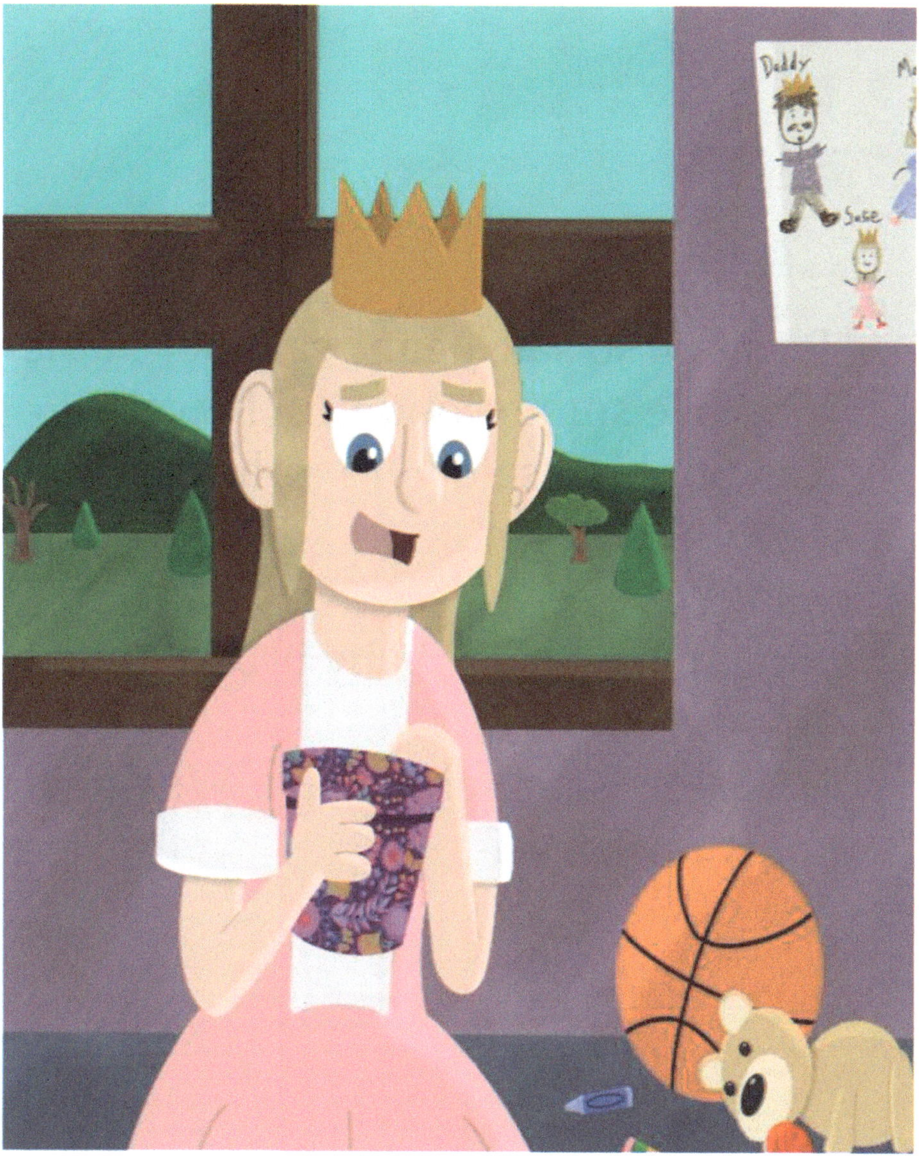
Daddy
Suse

"Don't be so sad, dear," said her Father. "We have some wonderful news!"
"Yes, Sophie," said her Mother. "'You see.. am with
child! You're
going to have your baby brother after all."
"Or sister" said her Father. "We don't know for sure if-

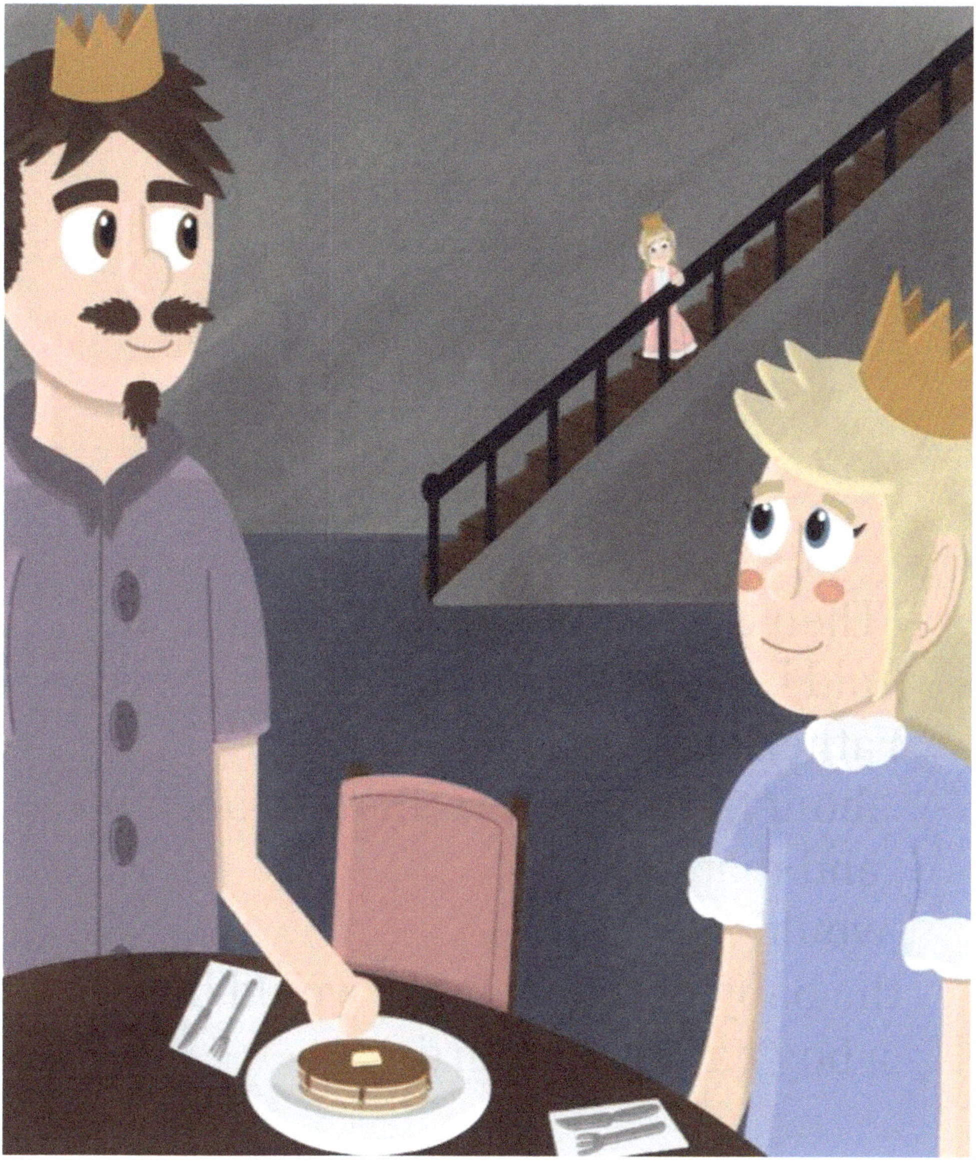

"Then it worked!" said Susie. And she told her Mother and
Father
 about the adventure she had been on
, and that not only
 would
the baby be a boy, but it would be
 a boy named Bernard.

Her parents, of-course, thought it was just pretend, or
a dream
shed had, or something like that, because parents tend not to
know about magic and instead use big words like
 "imagination" to try and explain things they don't understand.

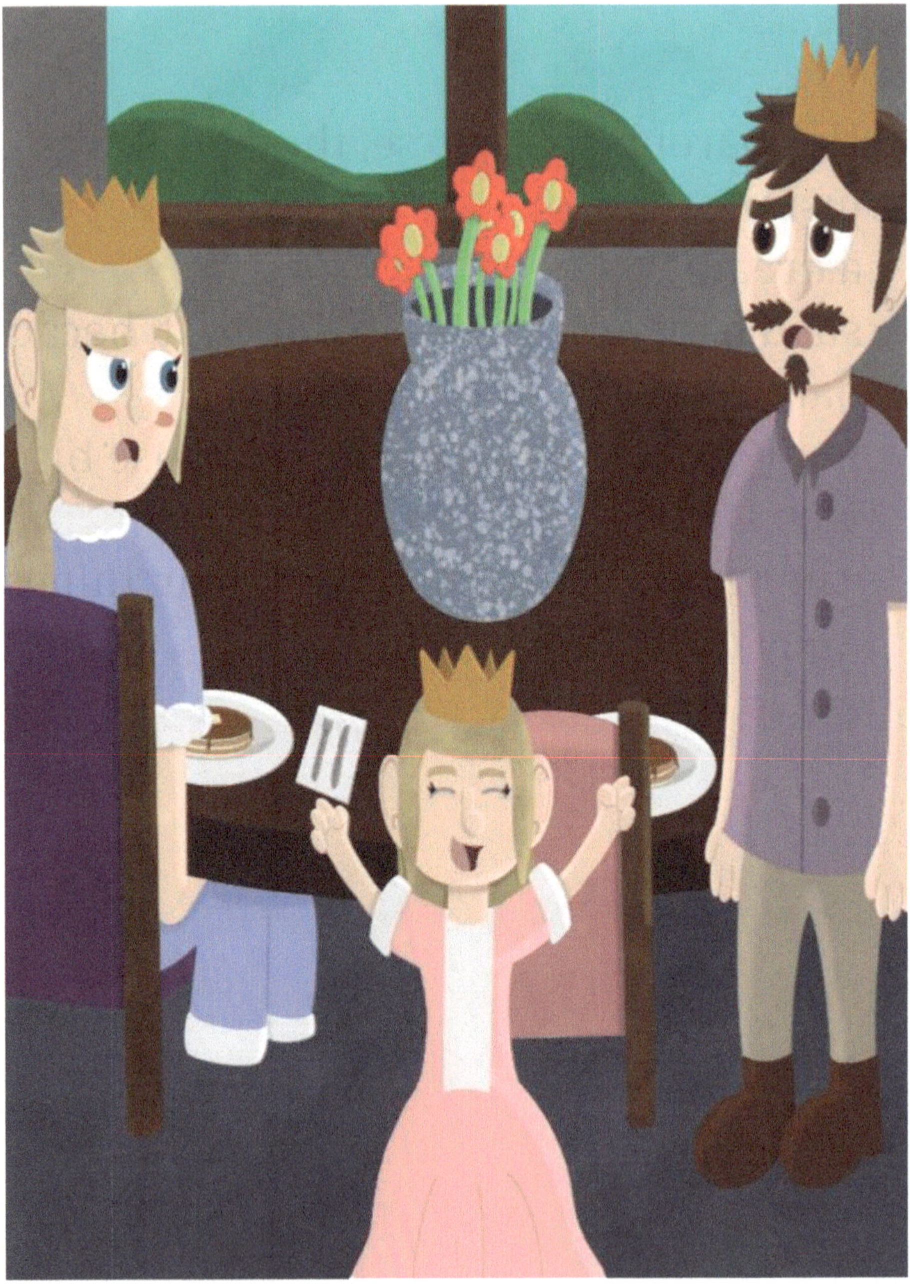

But none of that mattered, really. What did matter is that,
the usual number of months later, the Queen gave birth
 to a beautiful baby boy. And since Susie had been referring
to the unborn baby as Bernard all this time, it seemed logical
 to name the child Bernard.

The Kingdom rejoiced at the birth of
 Prince Bernard, the
Bunnies started a Milk And Cookies
Club for the other animals
 in the Big, scary Forest.

The liger gave up being mean and
 scary forever and just went around being
 nice to people so
 they would hug him,

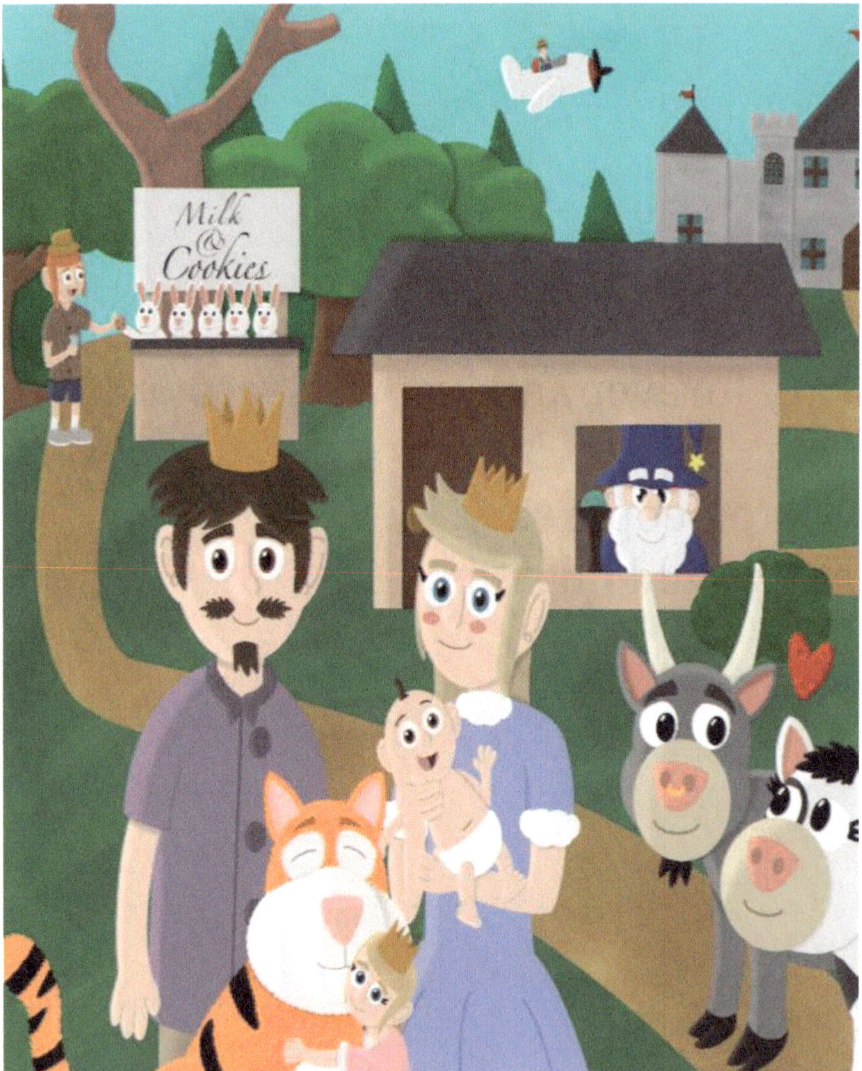
Milk & Cookies

Tyrone won a contest and took a trip
 to
Zimbabwe, Estelle met a handsome
bull and settled
 down, Gus moved
 out of the bush and into a house,
and everyone pretty
much went ahead and lived

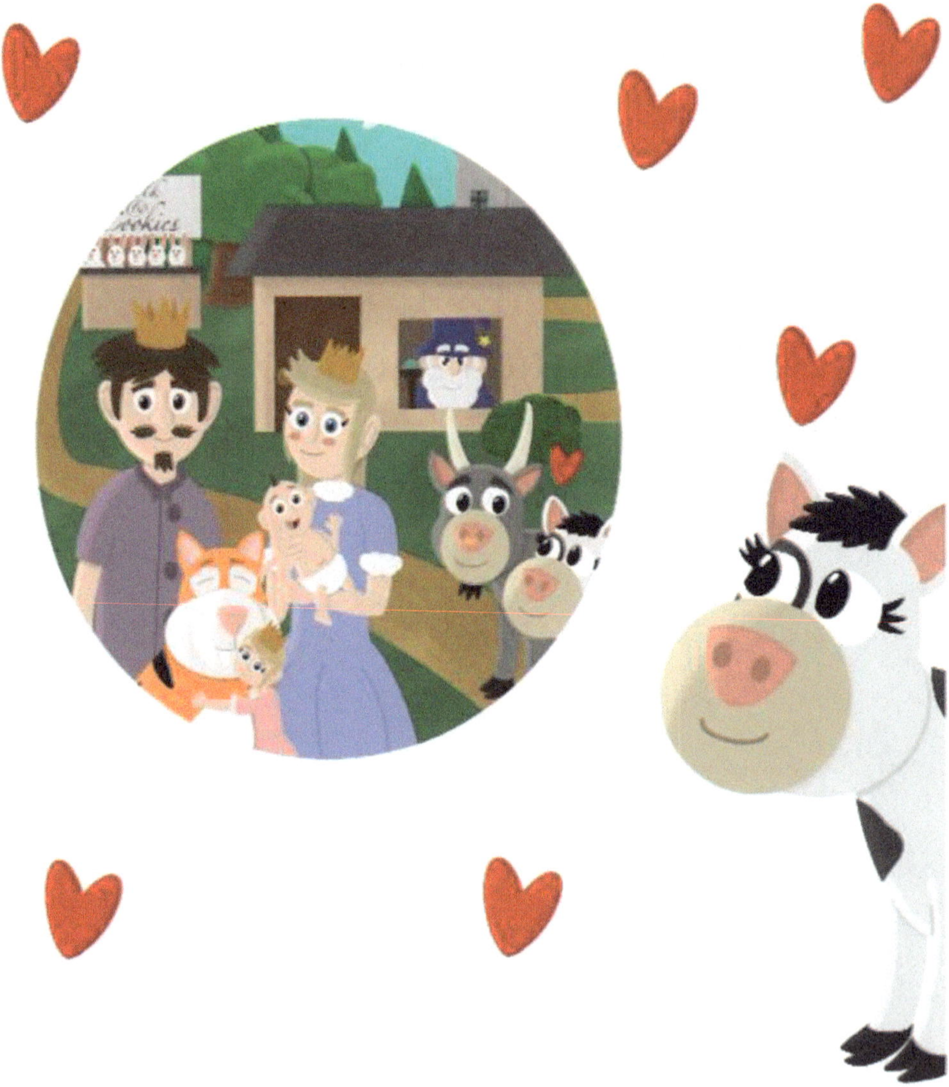

Happily Ever After

THE END